D1249803

track & field

the
SUMMER OLYMPICS

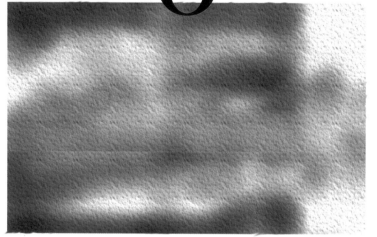

track&field

SUMMER OLYMPICS

PUBLISHED BY SMART APPLE MEDIA

Published by Smart Apple Media
123 South Broad Street, Mankato, Minnesota 56001

Cover Illustration by Eric Melhorn

Designed by Core Design

Photos by: Bettmann Archives, Sports Photo Masters
and Wide World Photos

Library of Congress Cataloging-in-Publication Data

Smale, David.
Track and field / by David Smale.
(The Summer Olympics)
Includes index.
Summary: Provides an overview of track and field
competition at the Olympics.

ISBN 1-887068-01-5

1. Track-athletics—Juvenile literature. 2. Olympics—
Juvenile literature. [1. Track and field—History. 2.
Olympics.] I. Title. II. Series.

GV1060.5.S53 1995   95-11963
796.4'2—dc20

"SWIFTER, HIGHER, STRONGER"

Of all the sports contested at the modern Olympic Games, one of the most popular is track and field. Speed, power, endurance, flexibility—track and field events demand all of these qualities from the athletes who participate in them. Track and field truly embodies the Olympic motto of "Citius, Altius, Fortius," which is Latin for "Swifter, Higher, Stronger." In fact, through-

The all-out 100-meter dash determines the swiftest runner.

Carl Lewis sails through the air in the long jump competition.

out most of the world, and in all international competition, the sport simply is called "athletics."

The original Olympics, held in ancient Greece, consisted solely of track and field events. Competitors battled for the olive wreath in long and short races and exhibitions of strength. Today the track events consist of 11 individual running events ranging from short dashes to the marathon, and also including two hurdle races and the steeplechase. Two relay races and two walks complete the track events. The field events consist of three jumps (long jump, triple jump and high jump), four throws (shot put, discus, javelin and hammer) and the pole vault. Finally, there are the multiple events—the decathlon for men and the heptathlon for women—that determine the "world's greatest athletes."

With only a short time before the next Olympics in Atlanta in 1996, there is much anticipation about who will become the star of the centennial Games. Will it be an aging champion who has one last shining moment? Or will there be a new star on the horizon?

SPRINTS, RELAYS AND HURDLES

Sprints are short-distance running events in which the competitors run at top speed for the entire race. Relays are events in which four teammates each sprint the same distance consecutively,

The high jump requires sprinting speed and agility (pages 10-11).

passing a baton from one to another. Hurdle races are sprints in which the athletes jump over evenly spaced barriers.

In women's competition, the Americans have dominated these events, although the African nations had a strong showing in Barcelona in 1992 and look to be even stronger in 1996. Evelyn Ashford is one of America's great sprinters, winning four gold medals for the United States (4 x 100-meter relay in 1984, 1988 and 1992, and 100-meter dash in 1984). Another is Florence Griffith

Evelyn Ashford sprints across the finish line.

Joyner, who broke the world record in the 100-meter dash in 1988 with a time of 10.49 seconds. She won a silver medal in the 200-meter dash in 1984 and a gold in the 100-meter dash in 1988.

The men's sprints also have been dominated by the Americans. From Thomas Burke, the first 100-meter champion in 1896 in Athens, to Jesse Owens, the hero of the 1936 Olympics in Berlin, to Carl Lewis, the two-time champion in 1984 and 1988, the Americans practically have owned the sprints.

MIDDLE AND LONG DISTANCES

The middle distances do not hold the glamour of the sprints or the stamina of the long events. But ever since England's Roger Bannister broke the 4-minute mile in 1954, the 1,500-meter

Kip Keino was one of the early stars of the middle distance races.

run, or "metric mile," has held a special place in the hearts of track fans.

The middle distances have had a wide range of strong competitors. The African nations, such as Kenya and Ethiopia, have been strong for the past 30 years, beginning in the late 1960s, when Kenyan Kip Keino defeated American Jim Ryun in 1968 in Mexico City in the most anticipated 1,500-meter run ever.

Olympians demonstrate strength and speed.

The 3,000-meter steeplechase, which is run by men only, has its origins in warrior cross-country pursuit. It includes hurdles over the dry track and a water jump (a permanent hurdle followed by a water pit) and covers a distance of nearly two miles. It is an obscure event with the most famous champion being Kip Keino in 1972.

The most famous long-distance race is the marathon. Its strange length (26 miles, 385 yards--42,195 m) comes from the legend of Pheidippides, a Greek soldier who, during a war against the Persians, ran from Marathon to Athens with a message of victory. After traveling the 26 miles and 385 yards between the two cities and telling the king of the news, he collapsed and died.

The Europeans always have done well in the long-distance races. Two Finns are among the all-time greats. Paavo Nurmi won many Olympic medals beginning in 1920. By the time his career was over, "The Flying Finn" had set world records 29 times in events ranging from 1,500 meters all the way up to 20,000 meters. The "Flying Finn" nickname was revived in the 1970s when Lasse Viren won the 5,000 and 10,000 in Munich in 1972 and followed that with victories in both events in 1976 in Montreal.

The men have been running the long distances since the renewal of the modern Olympics, while the women have added events through the years. The women ran their first Olympic marathon in 1984. At the U.S. Olympic Trials in 1984, Joan Benoit

won the race by 400 meters over Grete Waitz of Norway—despite having undergone knee surgery 17 days earlier. She then went on to claim Olympic gold in Los Angeles.

THE THROWS

The shot put, discus and hammer throw are strength events. The shot is a 16-pound (7.26 kg) iron or brass ball that is thrust through the air after being held just under the chin. It is a

Joan Benoit celebrates her marathon win with a victory lap.

movement that requires a tremendous amount of strength. A throw of 70 feet (21 meters) is considered extremely good. The Eastern European countries have dominated this event since the 1970s.

In the discus, competitors spin in a circle before throwing a 4 1/2-pound (2 kg) disc through the air. No one has dominated this event like American Al Oerter. Oerter is the only person in Olympic history to win the same track and field event in four consecutive games, winning in 1956, 1960, 1964 and 1968, setting Olympic records in each competition.

The javelin is a long spear made of wood or metal. In 1986, the International Amateur Athletics Federation moved the balance point and grip to cut down on dangerously long throws. The new aerodynamics make the javelin harder to throw. The gold-medal-winning distance decreased from 284 feet 8 inches (86.76 m) in 1984 to 276 feet 6 inches (84.27 m) in 1988.

The hammer throw involves a 16-pound (7.26 kg) metal sphere connected to a spring steel wire about 4 feet long (1.22 m). It has its origins in sledgehammer throwing in 15th- and 16th-century England. The United States dominated this event in the early Olympics, winning every gold medal through 1924, but has won only one gold medal since then.

JUMPS AND VAULT

The long jump is a simple event in which the athletes run at top speed down a track before leaping into a sand pit. The triple jump involves the same running approach, but then adds a hop on the same foot as the takeoff, then a step and a leap into the pit.

Al Oerter demonstrates Olympic form in the discus throw.

Pole vaulters sprint down a runway and propel themselves into the air with a pole, attempting to clear a bar in excess of 18 feet without dislodging it from its mounts. The pole vault is an event that lends itself to turnover. Only American Bob Richards has won more than one gold medal in the history of Olympic pole vaults. Richards won in 1952 in Helsinki and in 1956 in Melbourne. He also claimed the bronze medal in 1948 in London.

In the high jump, the jumper approaches a bar and attempts to clear it with the entire body, unaided by any outside apparatus. The story of the high jump was changed forever in 1968 when American Dick Fosbury cleared the bar on his back, rather than the conventional method of curling over the bar. To-

22

The Fosbury Flop (above).

Bob Beamon maintains control after his world-record-shattering jump.

day, most world-class high jumpers do "the Fosbury Flop."

The long jump, triple jump and pole vault didn't generate much attention in the early Olympic Games. But that all changed in the mid-1960s. Actually, one giant leap threw the jumps into the international spotlight. In 1968, American Bob Beamon leaped 29 feet 2 1/2 inches (8.9 m), breaking a world record by 1 foot 9 3/4 inches (55.25 cm) in an event where records are set by fractions of an inch. His world long jump record stood for 23 years, one of the longest runs for any world record in track and field history.

THE MULTI-EVENTS

The decathlon (for men) and the heptathlon (for women) determine the "world's greatest athletes." The 10 events of the decathlon are: the 100-meter dash, long jump, shot put, high jump, 400-meter dash, 110-meter hurdles, discus, pole vault, javelin and 1,500-meter run. The seven events of the heptathlon are: the 100-meter hurdles, high jump, shot-put, 200-meter dash, long jump, javelin and 800-meter run. Points are awarded in each event and are based on how close an athlete gets to the existing world record for that event.

Jackie Joyner-Kersee (Florence Griffith Joyner's sister-in-law) won the last two Olympic heptathlons and has recorded most of the top performances in the event's history. Among men, the

Powering through the hurdles (pages 26-27).

greatest multiple-event star was Jim Thorpe, who won the decathlon in the 1912 Olympics. His point total would have won the event in 1904, 1920 and 1924, and would have claimed the silver as late as 1948.

MORE EXCITEMENT AROUND THE CORNER

As the world approaches the 100th anniversary of the modern Olympics in Atlanta in 1996, track and field remains a prominent arena in which to achieve fame. Athletes will seek to break barriers of human performance: to jump more than 30 feet (9.1 m) in the long jump or higher than 8 feet (2.4 m) in the high jump; run the 100-meter dash faster than 9.8 seconds or the mile faster than 3:30; earn more than 9,000 points in the decathlon or 7,500 points in the heptathlon.

The women's 3000-meter run is a grueling race.

Who will be the new heroes? Only time—and height and distance—will tell. "Swifter, Higher, Stronger" will remain the goal for all the athletes.

Celebrating at the finish line.

track & field

RECORDS

Men

Event	Winner	Nation	Time (hour:min:sec) or distance
100-meter dash	Jim Hines	USA	0:09.90
200-meter dash	Joe DeLoach	USA	0:19.75
400-meter run	Quincy Watts	USA	0:43.50
800-meter run	Joaquim Cruz	Brazil	1:43.00
1500-meter run	Sebastian Coe	USA	3:32.53
5000-meter run	Said Aouita	Morocco	13:05.59
10000-meter run	Brahim Boutaib	Morocco	27:21.46
Marathon	Carlos Lopes	Portugal	2:09:21.00
110-meter hurdles	Roger Kingdom	USA	0:12.98
400-meter hurdles	Kevin Young	USA	0:46.78
3000-meter steeplechase	Julius Kariuki	Kenya	8:05.51
400-meter relay	Marsh,Burrell, Mitchell,C. Lewis	USA	0:37.40
1600-meter relay	Valmon,Watts, Johnson,S. Lewis	USA	2:55.74
20-km walk	Josef Pribilinec	Czech.	1:19:57.00
50-km walk	Vyacheslav Ivanenko	USSR	3:38:29.00
High jump	Gennadi Avdeenko	USSR	7'9-1/2"(2.38m)
Long jump	Bob Beamon	USA	29'2-1/2"(8.90m)
Triple jump	Mike Conley	USA	57'10-1/4"(17.63m)
Pole vault	Sergei Bubka	USSR	19'4-1/4"(5.90m)
Discus	Jurgen Schult	E.Germany	225'9-1/4"(68.82m)
Javelin	Jan Zelezny	Czech.	294'2" (89.66m)
Shot-put	Ulf Timmermann	E.Germany	73'8-3/4"(22.47m)
Hammer throw	Sergei Litvinov	USSR	278'2-1/2"(84.80m)
*Decathalon	Robert Zmelik	Czech.	8611 pts.

*1992 gold-medal winner

track & field

Women

Event	Winner	Nation	Time (hour:min:sec) or distance
100-meter dash	Florence Griffith Joyner	USA	0:10.54
200-meter dash	Florence Griffith Joyner	USA	0:21.34
400-meter run	Olga Bryzgina	USSR	0:48.65
800-meter run	Nadezhda Olizarenko	USSR	1:53.42
1500-meter run	Paula Ivan	Romania	3:53.96
3000-meter run	Tatiana Samolenko	USSR	8:26.53
10000-meter run	Olga Bondarenko	USSR	31:05.21
Marathon	Joan Benoit	USA	2:24:52.00
100-meter hurdles	Jordanka Donkova	Bulgaria	0:12.38
400-meter hurdles	Debra Flintoff-King	Australia	0:53.17
400-meter relay	Muller, Wockel, Auerswald, Gohr	E.Germany	0:41.60
1600-meter relay	Ledovskaia, Nazarova, Piniquina, Bryzgina	USSR	3:15.18
10-km walk	Chen Yueling	China	44:32.00
High jump	Louise Ritter	USA	6'8" (2.03m)
Long jump	Jackie Joyner-Kersee	USA	24'3-1/2"(7.40m)
Discus	Martina Hellmann	E.Germany	237'2-1/4"(72.30m)
Javelin	Petra Felke	E.Germany	245'0" (74.68m)
Shot-put	Ilona Slupianek	E.Germany	73'6-1/4"(22.41m)
*Heptathalon	Jackie Joyner-Kersee	USA	7044 pts.

*1992 gold-medal winner

INDEX